Let's Get

BARBECUE

Over **100** appetizing dishes

igloobooks

Published in 2017
by Igloo Books Ltd
Cottage Farm
Sywell
NN6 0BJ
www.igloobooks.com

Designed by Nicholas Gage
Edited by Jasmin Peppiatt

Food photography and recipe development
© Stockfood, The Food Media Agency
Additional imagery © iStock / Getty Images
Cover images: © iStock / Getty Images

LEO002 0417
2 4 6 8 10 9 7 5 3 1
ISBN 978-1-78557-444-3

Printed and manufactured in China

Contents

Meat Dishes 6

Fish Dishes 30

Fruit and Vegetable Dishes 48

Sides, Sauces and Desserts 62

Meat Dishes

SERVES: **4** | PREP TIME: **25-30 MINS** | COOKING TIME: **25 MINS**

Double Lamb Burger

2 small eggs

1 tbsp sunflower oil

1 tbsp unsalted butter

1 large onion, finely sliced

800 g / 1 lb 12 oz / 4 cups lamb mince

55 g / 2 oz / ½ cup Parmesan, finely grated

1 tsp Worcestershire sauce

salt and freshly ground black pepper

4 multiseed rolls, halved

100 g / 3 ½ oz / ½ cup tomato ketchup, to serve

1 small round lettuce, leaves torn

3 tbsp gherkin slices in vinegar, drained

oven chips, to serve

1. Cook the eggs in a large saucepan of boiling water for 12 minutes, then drain and refresh in iced water.

2. Preheat the barbecue to a moderately hot temperature.

3. Heat the oil and butter in a frying pan set over a moderate heat until hot.

4. Add the onion and a pinch of salt and sweat until softened, then continue to cook until golden at the edges. Set to one side.

5. Mix together the lamb mince, Parmesan, Worcestershire sauce and seasoning in a large mixing bowl.

6. Divide the mixture into eight and shape into burgers between your hands; make a thumb imprint in the centre of each patty before arranging on a rack or trivet.

7. Cook the burgers on the barbecue for 12–14 minutes, turning once, until firm yet slightly springy to the touch.

8. Meanwhile, peel the eggs and cut into slices.

9. Spread the bottom halves of the buns with a little ketchup, then top with lettuce and a cooked burger. Top with gherkin, a slice of egg and some onion before topping with another burger and more onion.

10. Serve with oven chips, with the tops of the buns and some tomato ketchup on the side.

SERVES: **4** | PREP TIME: **1 HOUR 30 MINS** | COOKING TIME: **45 MINS**

Sticky Tomato and Herb Ribs

1 rack spare ribs
500 ml / 17 ½ fl. oz / 2 cups red wine
2 tbsp olive oil
1 onion, finely chopped
2 cloves of garlic, crushed
1 red chilli, finely chopped
2 tbsp fresh thyme leaves
250 ml / 9 fl. oz / 1 cup tomato passata
2 tbsp coriander (cilantro) leaves, finely chopped

1. Cut the rib rack into sections to fit in a large saucepan and pour over the wine and 500 ml of water. Simmer gently for 1 hour, then leave to cool in the cooking liquid.
2. Meanwhile, heat the oil in a sauté pan and fry the onion, garlic, chilli and thyme for 10 minutes over a low heat.
3. Pour in the tomato passata and add a ladleful of the spare rib cooking liquor and simmer for 15 minutes.
4. Stir in the coriander, then transfer the sauce to a liquidizer and blend until smooth. Leave to cool.
5. Drain the ribs and pat dry with kitchen paper. Peel away the tough membrane from the back of the ribs. Brush liberally with the tomato sauce, then refrigerate until you are ready to cook.
6. Cook over a medium barbecue for 20 minutes, basting regularly with tomato sauce, until the glaze is lightly caramelised and the meat is piping hot all the way through.

Steak

2 x 400 g / 14 oz rib-eye steaks, trimmed
2 tbsp groundnut oil
salt and freshly ground black pepper

1. Preheat a barbecue to a moderately hot temperature.
2. Tie the steaks securely using butcher's twine so that they hold their shape.
3. Rub all over with groundnut oil and season generously with salt and pepper.
4. Grill on the barbecue for 4–7 minutes on each side depending on your desired cooking degree; the meat should feel firm yet springy to the touch when it is medium-rare.
5. Remove the steaks from the barbecue and leave them to rest, covered loosely with aluminium foil, for at least 10 minutes before serving.

Beer and Chilli Baby Ribs

2 racks baby back ribs, cut in half
1 litre / 1 pint 15 fl. oz / 4 cups beer
175 g / 6 oz / ½ cup chilli (chili) jam (jelly)

1. Put the rib racks in a saucepan with the beer and simmer very gently for 1 hour. Leave to cool completely in the cooking liquid.
2. Drain the ribs, then pat dry with kitchen paper. Peel away the tough membrane from the back of the ribs.
3. Brush liberally with chilli jam, then refrigerate until you are ready to cook.
4. Cook over a medium barbecue for 20 minutes, basting regularly with chilli jam, until the glaze is lightly caramelised and the meat is piping hot all the way through.

SERVES: 4 | PREP TIME: 15 MINS | COOKING TIME: 20 MINS

Rosemary Chicken with Puttanesca Sauce

4 skinless chicken breasts

50 ml / 1 ¾ fl. oz / ¼ cup olive oil

2 tbsp fresh rosemary, finely chopped, plus a few sprigs to garnish

2 cloves of garlic, crushed

4 anchovy fillets, finely chopped

1 tsp chilli (chili) flakes

400 g / 14 oz / 2 cups canned cherry tomatoes

2 tbsp capers

50 g / 1 ¾ oz / ⅓ cup pitted black olives

2 tbsp flat leaf parsley, finely chopped

1. Cut the chicken breasts in half horizontally with a sharp knife. Brush the chicken with 20 ml of the olive oil and sprinkle with rosemary, salt and pepper. Leave to marinate while you make the sauce.

2. Heat the rest of the oil in a sauté pan and fry the garlic, anchovy and chilli for 3 minutes.

3. Add the cherry tomatoes and simmer for 10 minutes. Stir in the capers and olives, then taste and adjust the seasoning.

4. Cook the chicken on a medium-hot barbecue for 3 minutes on each side or until the juices run clear.

5. Add a pool of Puttanesca sauce to four warm plates and sprinkle with parsley. Arrange the chicken on top and garnish with fresh rosemary.

SERVES: 4 | **PREP TIME: 30-45 MINS** | **COOKING TIME: 1 HOUR 15-20 MINS**

Pulled Pork Burger

2 tbsp sunflower oil

1 onion, finely chopped

3 cloves of garlic, minced

salt and freshly ground black pepper

1 tsp ground cumin

a pinch of ground cinnamon

a pinch of cayenne pepper

100 ml / 3 ½ fl. oz / ½ cup tomato ketchup

100 ml / 3 ½ fl. oz / ½ cup cider vinegar

2 tbsp soft dark brown sugar

450 ml / 16 fl. oz / 2 cups chicken stock

800 g / 1 lb 12 oz piece of pork shoulder, trimmed and scored

2 large carrots, peeled and shredded

½ small white cabbage, shredded

½ small red cabbage, shredded

110 g / 4 oz / ½ cup plain yogurt

75 g / 3 oz / ⅓ cup mayonnaise

a small handful of flat-leaf parsley, chopped

4 sesame seed buns, split

1. Heat the oil in a casserole dish set over a moderate heat until hot.
2. Add the onion, garlic and some seasoning; sweat until golden.
3. Add the spices and cook for a further minute before adding the ketchup, vinegar, sugar and chicken stock.
4. Bring to a simmer, stir well, then add the pork and cover. Cook at a steady simmer for 50–60 minutes, then remove from the sauce and pat dry.
5. Preheat the barbecue to a moderately hot temperature.
6. Mix together the shredded carrot and cabbages in a mixing bowl, then stir through the yogurt, half the mayonnaise and all of the parsley.
7. Season to taste before covering and chilling until ready to use.
8. Finish the pork on the barbecue for 15–20 minutes, turning frequently.
9. Continue to cook the barbecue sauce in the casserole dish until reduced and thickened.
10. Once the pork is ready, shred it using a fork, then stir it back into the barbecue sauce, leaving to absorb for 10 minutes.
11. Toast the burger buns on the barbecue, then spread the bottom halves with the left over mayonnaise.
12. Top with the pork in barbecue sauce followed by the coleslaw; add the tops of the buns before serving.

SERVES: 4 | PREP TIME: 10-15 MINS | COOKING TIME: 8-10 MINS

Chicken, Beef and Chorizo Skewers

2 large skinless chicken breasts
400 g / 14 oz rump steak, trimmed
6 small chorizo sausages
3 tbsp olive oil
½ tsp cumin seeds
a small bunch of thyme, roughly chopped
1 large onion, thickly sliced
salt and freshly ground black pepper
tomato salsa, to serve
lime wedges, to serve

1. Preheat the barbecue to a moderately hot temperature and soak six wooden skewers in water.
2. Cut the chicken breasts and steak into large chunks and add to a mixing bowl with the chorizo.
3. Add the oil, cumin seeds, thyme, onion and seasoning. Mix everything well until coated, then thread three chorizo sausages each onto two skewers.
4. Thread the chicken pieces onto two wooden skewers and then the steak onto the remaining skewers, along with the slices of onions.
5. Drizzle any remaining oil from the bowl over the skewers, then grill on the barbecue for 8–10 minutes, turning once halfway through cooking.
6. Serve the skewers with pots of salsa and lime wedges on the side.

SERVES: 4 | PREP TIME: 15 MINS | COOKING TIME: 10-12 MINS

Beefburger

600 g / 1 lb 5 oz / 3 cups steak mince
salt and freshly ground black pepper
6 rashers of bacon
100 g / 3 ½ oz / ½ cup mayonnaise
1 tbsp tomato ketchup
a dash of Worcestershire sauce
1 little gem lettuce, leaves separated
4 burger buns, split
1 vine tomato, sliced
1 red onion, thinly sliced
1 tbsp sliced gherkins in vinegar, drained
1 red pepper, sliced

1. Preheat the barbecue to a moderately hot temperature.
2. Place the steak mince in a large bowl and add a generous amount of salt and pepper. Mix the seasoning into the mince, breaking it up with your hands.
3. Divide the mince into four and shape into patties between your hands; make a thumb imprint in the centre of each patty before arranging on the rack or trivet.
4. Cook on the barbecue for 10–12 minutes, turning once, until firm yet springy to the touch.
5. Meanwhile, cook the rashers of bacon on the barbecue for around 5–6 minutes until fully cooked and slightly crispy.
6. Whisk together the mayonnaise, ketchup and Worcestershire sauce with a little seasoning for a quick burger sauce.
7. Place a leaf of the gem lettuce on the bottom half of each bun and add a spoonful of the burger sauce, followed by the cooked burgers.
8. Top with a combination of bacon, tomato, red onion, gherkin and red pepper then add the burger bun tops. Serve immediately.

Lime and Honey Chicken Wings

2 limes
2 tbsp runny honey
2 tbsp fish sauce
1 tbsp sriracha chilli (chili) sauce
1 clove of garlic, crushed
1 tbsp sesame oil
12 chicken wings, jointed

1. Finely grate the zest of one of the limes and set it aside. Squeeze the juice and mix it with the honey, fish sauce, sriracha, garlic and sesame oil.
2. Tip the marinade into a sandwich bag and add the chicken wings. Massage well to coat and leave to marinate in the fridge for 2 hours.
3. Cook the chicken wings over a medium-hot barbecue for 20 minutes, turning occasionally. They are ready when the juices run clear and the skin is nicely charred.
4. Sprinkle the wings with lime zest and cut the other lime into large wedges to serve alongside.

Beer Can Chicken

1 tbsp smoked paprika
1 tsp golden caster (superfine) sugar
a pinch of ground cumin
salt and freshly ground black pepper
2 tbsp sunflower oil
1.5 kg / 3 lb 5 oz chicken, cleaned and trimmed
400 ml / 14 fl. oz can of beer or lager

1. Preheat the barbecue to a moderate temperature – around 200°C / 400F. It is important that your barbecue has a lid that will easily cover the chicken when it is cooking upright.
2. Mix together the paprika, sugar, cumin and seasoning to make a dry rub.
3. Add the sunflower oil slowly and stir until you have a paste-like consistency before massaging into the chicken.
4. Open the can of beer and pour half into a glass; lower the cavity of the chicken over and onto the can of beer.
5. Sit the beer can and chicken upright on the barbecue and cover carefully with the lid.
6. Roast the chicken for 1 hour 10–20 minutes until the meat pulls away from the bone and juices run clear when the thickest part of the thigh is pierced.
7. Carefully remove the chicken from the barbecue and cover it loosely with a piece of aluminium foil. Leave to rest for 10 minutes before serving.

Sharing Sirloin

700 g / 1 lb 8 oz well-hung sirloin steak
2 tbsp olive oil
1 dried red chilli (chili), pierced with a knife
1 sprig rosemary
1 clove of garlic, skin left on and squashed
a pinch of rock salt

1. Put the steak in a large sandwich bag with the oil, chilli, rosemary and garlic. Marinate in the fridge for 4 hours.
2. Remove the steak from the marinade and pat dry with kitchen paper. Season liberally with rock salt.
3. Prepare the barbecue with the coals on one side and ensure the metal grill is very hot. Cook the steak directly over the coals for 3 minutes on each side, then transfer to the side without coals. Put a small metal bowl of water next to it on the coals side, then cover with a lid and cook for 8 minutes.
4. Transfer the steak to a chopping board and cover with a double layer of foil and a dry tea towel.
5. Leave to rest for 5 minutes before slicing and serving.

Turkey and Vegetable Skewers

1 turkey breast, cut into 32 chunks
1 large onion, cubed
1 red pepper, cubed
1 green pepper, cubed
2 tbsp olive oil
2 tbsp sundried tomato paste
1 clove of garlic, crushed
1 tbsp lemon juice

1. Soak eight wooden skewers in cold water for 20 minutes.
2. Thread the turkey and vegetables onto the skewers and set aside.
3. Mix the oil with the sundried tomato paste, garlic and lemon juice and season with salt and pepper.
4. Thoroughly brush the mixture over the turkey and vegetables and leave to marinate for 1 hour.
5. Cook over a medium-hot barbecue for 15 minutes, turning regularly to ensure the meat is cooked through evenly.

SERVES: **4** | PREP TIME: **10 MINS** | COOKING TIME: **15-17 MINS**

Blackened Chicken

4 medium chicken breasts, trimmed
2 tsp dried oregano
2 tsp dried thyme
1 tsp onion powder
1 tsp garlic powder
1 tsp smoked paprika
½ tsp cayenne pepper
55 ml / 2 fl. oz / ¼ cup sunflower oil
a small bunch of salad (green) onions, halved
2 green chillies (chilies)
1 small green pepper, finely diced
salt and freshly ground black pepper

1. Preheat the barbecue to a moderately hot temperature.
2. Cut a few slashes in the chicken breasts and place in a mixing bowl.
3. Whisk together the dried herbs and ground spices with half of the oil until paste-like in consistency; add a little water if it's too dry. Evenly coat the chicken breasts with the paste.
4. Grill the chicken breasts, skin-side down to begin with until blackened, before turning and leaving to finish cooking. The chicken should register at least 74°C / 165F on a meat thermometer.
5. Remove the chicken from the barbecue and leave to rest for 5 minutes, covered loosely with aluminium foil.
6. Drizzle the onions and chillies with the remaining oil; season well, then grill on the barbecue until lightly charred.
7. Serve the chicken alongside the grilled vegetables, garnished with a sprinkle of diced green pepper.

SERVES: 4 | PREP TIME: 25 MINS | COOKING TIME: 14-16 MINS

Sweet and Sour Chicken Wings

55 g / 2 oz / ¼ cup runny honey
55 ml / 2 fl. oz / ¼ cup distilled vinegar
1 tbsp light soy sauce
2 tbsp sunflower oil
2 tbsp water
a pinch of dried chilli (chili) flakes
salt and freshly ground pepper
900 g / 2 lb chicken wings, cleaned with tips removed

1. Preheat the barbecue to a moderately hot temperature.
2. Whisk together the honey, vinegar, soy sauce, sunflower oil, water, chilli flakes and seasoning until smooth.
3. Add the wings to the marinade and leave for 15 minutes.
4. Shake off any excess marinade, then arrange the wings evenly on the barbecue.
5. Cook for 14–16 minutes, turning frequently, until golden and sticky on the outside.
6. Leave the wings to rest for 5 minutes before serving.

SERVES: **4** | PREP TIME: **15 MINS** | COOKING TIME: **8-10 MINS**

Lamb and Beef Skewers

2 tbsp sunflower oil

2 tbsp water

1 tbsp tomato purée

1 tbsp honey

a dash of Worcestershire sauce

a small handful of basil leaves, finely chopped

salt and freshly ground black pepper

450 g / 1 lb lamb neck fillet, trimmed

450 g / 1 lb rump steak, trimmed

1. Preheat the barbecue to a moderately hot temperature and soak eight wooden skewers in cold water for 30 minutes.
2. Whisk together the sunflower oil, water, tomato purée, honey, Worcestershire sauce, basil and seasoning in a mixing bowl.
3. Cut the lamb and beef into bite-sized chunks, then add to the marinade. Coat well and leave for 10 minutes.
4. Brush off any excess marinade before threading the meat onto the wooden skewers.
5. Grill on the barbecue for 8–10 minutes, turning once halfway through, until the meat is firm yet slightly springy to the touch.
6. Remove from the barbecue and leave to rest for 5 minutes before serving.

Chicken Kebabs

2 courgettes (zucchinis)
2 large skinless chicken breasts, trimmed
2 tbsp sunflower oil
2 tbsp light soy sauce
2 tsp red peppercorns, lightly crushed
1 lemon, cut into wedges

1. Soak 8 wooden skewers in cold water for 30 minutes.
2. Meanwhile, score the outsides of the courgettes at intervals and slice into thick coins.
3. Cook in a saucepan of salted, boiling water for 3–4 minutes until tender; drain and leave to cool to one side.
4. Preheat the barbecue to a moderately hot temperature.
5. Cut each chicken breast into four fingers and place in a large mixing bowl.
6. Add the sunflower oil, soy sauce and peppercorns; mix well to coat and leave for 10 minutes.
7. Thread the pieces of chicken onto the wooden skewers and cook on the barbecue for 7–9 minutes, turning once, until the chicken is firm yet very slightly springy to the touch.
8. Serve the kebabs with the courgette and lemon wedges on the side.

Shallot and Thyme Smoked Sausage

2 tbsp runny honey
1 tbsp Dijon mustard
400 g / 14 oz Cumberland ring sausage
2 tbsp butter
3 large shallots, halved
1 large bunch fresh thyme

1. Mix the honey with the mustard and brush the mixture over the sausage.
2. Heat the butter in a cast iron oven-proof frying pan and fry the shallots cut side down for 5 minutes over a low heat. Turn them over and scatter over the thyme. Place the sausage on top.
3. Transfer the pan to a medium-hot barbecue and sit a metal bowl of water next to it. Cover with a lid and hot-smoke the sausage for 30-40 minutes or until cooked all the way through.

SERVES: **4** | PREP TIME: **15-20 MINS** | COOKING TIME: **10-13 MINS**

Glazed Duck Breast

4 medium duck breasts, trimmed
75 g / 3 oz / ½ cup orange marmalade
1 orange, juiced
salt and freshly ground black pepper
4 figs, quartered
a few sprigs of rosemary, chopped

1. Preheat a barbecue to a moderately high temperature.
2. Using a sharp knife, make 5–6 shallow incisions in the skin of the duck breasts.
3. Lay the duck breasts skin-side down on the barbecue and cook over the heat until the fat has rendered away.
4. Mix together the marmalade, orange juice and plenty of seasoning in a small bowl.
5. Once the fat has rendered from the duck breasts and the skin starts to turn golden brown, flip them and brush their tops with the orange glaze.
6. Continue cooking for 5–8 minutes depending on your cooking preference.
7. Remove the duck breasts from the barbecue when ready and leave them to rest on a warm plate, covered loosely with aluminium foil.
8. Place a sauté pan over a medium heat and add a good splash of water along with the figs and a little of the marmalade glaze.
9. Cook the figs until softened, then serve alongside the duck breasts, garnished with rosemary.

MAKES: **6** | PREP TIME: **30 MINS** | COOKING TIME: **15 MINS**

Chicken, Sausage and Vegetable Kebabs

1 chicken breast, cut into 12 chunks

3 sausages, quartered

1 red onion, cut into wedges

1 courgette (zucchini), sliced

½ red pepper, cut into chunks

½ yellow pepper, cut into chunks

2 tbsp fresh rosemary, finely chopped, plus a few sprigs to garnish

1 tbsp pink peppercorns, crushed

2 tsp coriander seeds, crushed

50 ml / 1 ¾ fl. oz / ¼ cup olive oil

1. Soak six wooden skewers in cold water for 20 minutes.
2. Thread the chicken, sausage and vegetables onto the skewers and set aside.
3. Mix the rosemary, pink pepper and coriander together then set aside a third of the mixture. Stir the rest into the oil and season with salt and pepper.
4. Brush the kebabs with the spiced oil and cook over a medium-hot barbecue for 15 minutes, turning regularly.
5. Sprinkle the kebabs with the rest of the spice mix and serve immediately, garnished with rosemary.

SERVES: 4 | PREP TIME: 25 MINS | COOKING TIME: 10-14 MINS

Grilled Pork Chops

2 limes
2 tbsp sunflower oil
3 tbsp silver tequila
1 ½ tbsp agave nectar
3 tbsp water
4 x 300 g / 10 ½ oz bone-in pork chops, trimmed
a small bunch of flat-leaf parsley, chopped
salt and freshly ground black pepper

1. Preheat the barbecue to a moderately hot temperature.
2. Juice one of the limes into a mixing bowl before whisking in the sunflower oil, tequila, agave nectar, water and seasoning. Cut the other lime into wedges.
3. Coat the pork chops in the mixture and leave to marinate for 15 minutes.
4. Let the excess marinade drip off the pork chops then grill for 5–7 minutes on both sides until the centre of the chops read 63°C / 145F on a meat thermometer.
5. Remove the chops from the barbecue and leave to rest for 5 minutes before garnishing with chopped parsley and lime wedges.

Chilli Oil Chicken

4 skinless chicken breasts
3 tbsp chilli (chili) oil

1. Put the chicken breasts between two sheets of clingfilm and bat them out lightly with a rolling pin until they are approximately 1.5cm (½ in) thick. This will help them to cook quickly and evenly on the barbecue.
2. Discard the clingfilm and brush the chicken with chilli oil, then leave to marinate in the fridge for at least 1 hour.
3. Cook the chicken breasts on a medium-hot barbecue for 2 minutes, then turn them 90° and cook for another 2 minutes to make the classic criss-cross pattern.
4. Turn over the chicken breasts and repeat. Pierce the centre of the chicken with a skewer – if the juices run clear, it is ready.

Mediterranean Chicken Sausages

1.2 kg / 2 lb 10 oz / 8 ⅓ cups chicken thigh, chopped
2 cloves of garlic, crushed
2 lemons, zest finely grated
50 g / 1 ¾ oz / ½ cup Parmesan, finely grated
50 g / 1 ¾ oz / ½ cup sundried tomato paste
a small bunch basil, chopped
natural sausage casings

1. Put all of the ingredients in a food processor and pulse until finely chopped and evenly mixed.
2. Fill the sausage casings with the mixture using a sausage machine or a large piping bag, ensuring you eliminate any air pockets. Twist into 12 sausages and snip with scissors to separate.
3. Leave the sausages to rest in the fridge for 4 hours.
4. Barbecue the sausages over medium-low coals for 20 minutes, turning regularly. Make sure they are piping hot throughout before serving.

SERVES: **4** | PREP TIME: **30-45 MINS** | COOKING TIME: **40-45 MINS**

Pork Ribs

55 ml / 2 fl. oz / ¼ cup dark rum
75 g / 3 oz / ⅓ cup Demerara (Turbinado) sugar
75 ml / 3 fl. oz / ⅓ cup dark soy sauce
55 g / 2 oz / ¼ cup runny honey
2 cloves of garlic, minced
1 tbsp Dijon mustard
1 tbsp tomato purée
a pinch of cayenne pepper
freshly ground black pepper
1 kg / 2 lb 4 oz pork spare ribs

1. Preheat the barbecue to a moderately hot temperature and preheat the oven to 180°C (160°C fan) / 350F / gas 4 at the same time.
2. Whisk together the rum, sugar, soy sauce, honey, garlic, mustard, tomato purée, cayenne and plenty of black pepper in a small mixing bowl.
3. Pour the sauce over the ribs and massage into them using your hands; leave them to sit for 15 minutes.
4. Brush any excess marinade off the ribs and reserve, then place the ribs on a baking tray; cook in the oven for 30 minutes.
5. Remove the ribs after 30 minutes and brush with the reserved marinade, then finish on the barbecue for 10–15 minutes until sticky and starting to form a crust.
6. Remove them from the barbecue and leave to rest for 10 minutes before slicing and serving.

Shredded Barbecue Pork Buns

2 ½ tsp fennel seeds
½ tsp cumin seeds
½ tsp black peppercorns
½ tsp coriander seeds
1 tsp garlic granules
1 tsp dried oregano
50 g / 1 ¾ oz / ¼ cup smoked sea salt
50 g / 1 ¾ oz / ¼ cup soft dark
   brown sugar

25 g / 1 oz / 1/8 cup granulated sugar
1 tbsp smoked paprika
1 tsp cayenne
2 kg / 4 lb 6 oz pork shoulder, from the
   collar end
12 burger buns, halved horizontally
12 slices cheese
barbecue sauce, coleslaw and pickles,
   to serve

1. Toast the whole spices in a dry pan, then cool. Grind in a spice grinder with the
   garlic granules, oregano and salt. Mix in the sugars, smoked paprika and cayenne.
2. Rub the mixture into the pork and leave to marinate overnight. Remove from the
   fridge 2 hours before cooking.
3. Put a pile of charcoal on one side of the barbecue and top it with wood chips.
   Light a large handful of coals in a chimney starter and burn until the flames die
   down. Tip them onto the wood chips and place a metal tray of water on the
   empty side.
4. Fit the grill rack and position the pork over the water tray. Put on the lid and open
   the top and bottom vents half way.
5. Smoke the pork for 5 hours or until it reaches an internal temperature of
   65°C / 150F.
6. Wrap the pork tightly with foil and top up the charcoal if needed. Replace the lid
   and open the top and bottom vents fully.
7. Cook for 5 hours or until the pork reaches 93°C / 200F. Leave to rest in a warm
   place for 45 minutes.
8. Pull the pork and add a little barbecue sauce if liked. Add a slice of cheese to each
   bun and top with pork, then garnish with your choice of coleslaw and pickles.

SERVES: 4 | PREP TIME: 10 MINS | COOKING TIME: 25 MINS

Grilled Toulouse Sausages

2 tbsp sunflower oil

1 tbsp unsalted butter

1 large red onion, finely sliced

2 large carrots, peeled and cut into thin discs

110 ml / 4 fl. oz / ½ cup red wine

250 ml / 9 fl. oz / 1 cup beef stock

1 tbsp caster (superfine) sugar

4 large Toulouse sausages

salt and freshly ground black pepper

a few sprigs of chervil, to garnish

1. Preheat a barbecue to a moderately high temperature.
2. Heat together the sunflower oil and butter in a large saucepan set over a moderate heat.
3. Add the red onion and carrots and sweat with a little salt for 4–5 minutes.
4. Deglaze the pan with the red wine and let it reduce by half, then add the beef stock and sugar.
5. Bring to a boil, then reduce the heat slightly and add the sausages.
6. Cook the sausages for 10 minutes, then remove them from the sauce and pat dry. Leave the sauce to continue reducing over a low heat, adjusting the seasoning to taste.
7. Place the sausages on the barbecue and cook for 3–4 minutes on both sides until lightly charred.
8. Serve with the carrot and onion sauce spooned over and a garnish of chervil on top.

Pork and Beef Burgers

225 g / 8 oz / 1 cup minced beef
225 g / 8 oz / 1 cup pork sausagemeat
2 tbsp double (heavy) cream
1 tsp Dijon mustard
1 tsp smoked paprika
4 sesame burger buns, halved horizontally
4 slices cheese
mixed salad to serve

1. Mix the mince and sausagemeat with the cream, mustard and paprika and season generously with salt and pepper.
2. Knead lightly until sticky then divide the mixture into four and shape into patties. Chill until you're ready to cook.
3. Barbecue the burgers over medium-hot coals for 4 minutes on each side. Briefly toast the cut side of the buns, then add a slice of cheese to each one and top with salad and the burgers. Serve immediately.

Spicy Apple Chicken Skewers

3 skinless chicken breasts
1 red chilli (chili), finely chopped
1 spring onion (scallion), finely chopped
1 tbsp flat leaf parsley, finely chopped
1 clove of garlic, crushed
½ lime, zest finely grated
3 tbsp olive oil
2 apples, peeled, cored and cut
  into chunks

1. Cut each chicken breast into eight cubes.
2. Mix the chilli, spring onion, parsley, garlic and lime zest with the oil and season with salt and pepper. Toss the mixture with the chicken and leave to marinate for at least 1 hour.
3. Meanwhile, soak six wooden skewers in cold water for 20 minutes.
4. Thread the chicken onto the skewers, alternating with the apple chunks.
5. Cook the skewers over a medium-low barbecue for 20 minutes or until cooked through, turning regularly.

SERVES: 4 | PREP TIME: **10-15 MINS** | COOKING TIME: **1 HOUR 30 MINS-2 HOURS**

Beef Ribs in Barbecue Sauce

2 x 600 g / 1 lb 5 oz centre-cut beef ribs, trimmed
3 tbsp sunflower oil
150 g / 5 oz / ⅔ cup tomato ketchup
75 ml / 3 fl. oz / ⅓ cup rice wine vinegar
2 tbsp cider vinegar
75 g / 3 oz / ½ cup dark brown soft sugar
a dash of Worcestershire sauce
½ tsp mustard powder
a pinch of cayenne pepper
salt and freshly ground black pepper

1. Preheat the barbecue to a moderately low temperature – around 140°C / 275F.
2. Brush the ribs with the sunflower oil and season generously.
3. Arrange the ribs on the barbecue and cook for 1 ½–2 hours until the meat is extremely tender.
4. As the ribs cook, prepare the sauce by mixing together the ketchup, vinegars, sugar, Worcestershire sauce, mustard powder, cayenne and seasoning in a small saucepan.
5. Bring the sauce to the boil, stirring frequently, then reduce to a simmer until thickened. Adjust the seasoning to taste.
6. Ten minutes before the ribs are ready, brush them with the barbecue sauce and continue to cook.
7. Remove the ribs from the barbecue and brush with more sauce before serving.

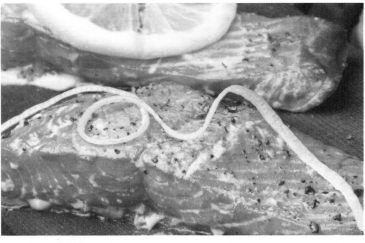

Fish Dishes

SERVES: 6 | PREP TIME: 2 HOURS 10 MINS | COOKING TIME: 20 MINS

Cedar Planked Salmon

6 portions skinless salmon fillet

3 tbsp maple syrup

1 tbsp Dijon mustard

a few sprigs rosemary

1 lemon, cut into wedges

1 lime, cut into wedges

salt and pepper

1. Soak two cedar wood planks in warm salted water for 2 hours.

2. Meanwhile, put the salmon in a large sandwich bag with the rest of the ingredients. Seal it up and leave to marinate in the fridge.

3. Set your barbecue up for indirect cooking, so that all of the coals are positioned to one side.

4. Arrange the salmon on the cedar planks with some of the rosemary, lemon and lime from the marinade. Season liberally with salt and black pepper.

5. Position the planks on the side of the barbecue with no coals, then cover the barbecue and cook for 20 minutes or until the salmon has only just turned opaque in the centre.

Prawn and Chorizo Brochettes

2 limes
110 ml / 4 fl. oz / ½ cup olive oil
1 red chilli (chili), chopped
2 cloves of garlic
1 tsp smoked paprika
salt and freshly ground black pepper
8 king prawns
100 g / 3 ½ oz piece of chorizo, peeled
1 tsp sesame seeds

1. Preheat the barbecue to a high temperature and soak eight mini wooden brochettes in cold water for 30 minutes.
2. Cut one of the limes in half and set to one side; juice the other.
3. Combine the oil, chilli, garlic, paprika, lime juice and seasoning in a food processor and blitz until smooth.
4. Peel and de-vein the prawns, keeping their tails intact, then cut the chorizo into eight coins.
5. Thread a prawn onto each skewer with a coin of chorizo between the head and tail.
6. Brush with some of the spicy oil and arrange on a grilling tray alongside the lime halves.
7. Grill on the barbecue for 2 minutes on each side until the prawns are pink and cooked through.
8. Remove from the grill and garnish with a sprinkling of sesame seeds, serving with the spicy oil and lime halves on the side.

SERVES: **4** | PREP TIME: **20 MINS** | COOKING TIME: **4-6 MINS**

Crab Cakes

400 g / 14 oz / 2 ⅔ cups canned white crabmeat, drained and picked through for bone

1 small red pepper, very finely diced

a small bunch of dill, finely chopped

1 tbsp mayonnaise

a pinch of cayenne pepper

1 small egg, beaten

salt and freshly ground black pepper

125 g / 4 ½ oz / 1 cup breadcrumbs

55 ml / 2 fl. oz / ¼ cup sunflower oil, plus extra for shaping mixed leaf salad, to garnish

1. Preheat a barbecue to a moderately hot temperature.

2. In a large mixing bowl, combine the crabmeat with the red pepper, dill, mayonnaise, cayenne pepper, egg, seasoning and a quarter of the breadcrumbs.

3. Mix well until you can take generous spoonfuls of the mixture and shape into eight patties between oiled hands.

4. Place the remaining breadcrumbs in a shallow dish and dip the patties into the breadcrumbs to coat.

5. Drizzle the crab cakes with a little oil, then cook on the barbecue, oiled side down, for 2–3 minutes until golden brown.

6. Lightly oil the uncooked side before flipping and cooking for another 2–3 minutes.

7. Carefully remove the crab cakes from the barbecue and drain on kitchen paper.

8. Serve immediately with the mixed leaf salad on the side.

Planked Lemon Sea Trout

600 g / 1 lb 5 oz sea trout fillet, taken from the thick end
2 tbsp runny honey
salt and pepper
1 lemon, sliced

1. Soak a cedar wood plank in warm salted water for 2 hours.
2. Spread the sea trout with honey and season with salt and pepper. Top with the lemon slices.
3. Toast the cedar plank over a medium-hot barbecue for 4 minutes or until it starts to smell smoky.
4. Turn over the plank and lay the sea trout on top, skin side down. Cover the barbecue with a lid and cook for 15 minutes or until the sea trout is just opaque in the centre.

Barbecued Sardines

12 sardine fillets, cleaned and gutted
sea salt and freshly ground black pepper
100 ml / 3 ½ fl. oz / ½ cup olive oil
1 lemon, juiced
4 lemon slices, to garnish

1. Preheat a barbecue to a moderately hot temperature.
2. Make diagonal slashes in the skin and flesh of the sardines, then season the insides with sea salt and black pepper.
3. Drizzle the olive oil over and rub well to coat evenly, before seasoning the outsides.
4. Barbecue the sardines for 8–10 minutes, turning once halfway through.
5. Remove the sardines from the barbecue once the flesh is firm and the skin is golden.
6. Drizzle with lemon juice before serving with lemon slices on top.

Prawn and Scallop Skewers

12 raw prawns, peeled with tails left intact

8 scallops, shelled

50 g / 1 ¾ oz / ¼ cup butter, melted

1 clove of garlic, crushed

1 lemon, juiced and zest finely grated

½ tsp ground coriander

2 tbsp fresh coriander (cilantro), finely chopped

1. Soak four wooden skewers in cold water for 20 minutes.
2. Thread the prawns and scallops onto the skewers.
3. Mix the butter with the garlic, lemon zest and ground coriander and season with salt and pepper. Brush the mixture over the skewers and leave to marinate for 30 minutes.
4. Cook the skewers over a hot barbecue for 2 minutes on each side or until the prawns and scallops are opaque in the centre and lightly charred on the outside.
5. Drizzle the skewers with lemon juice and serve scattered with chopped coriander.

SERVES: **4** | PREP TIME: **15 MINS** | COOKING TIME: **6-8 MINS**

Tuna Burger

600 g / 1 lb 5 oz tuna steak, chopped

75 g / 3 oz / ¾ cup pecorino,
  finely grated

a dash of fish sauce

a small bunch of flat-leaf parsley,
  chopped

salt and freshly ground black pepper

2–3 tbsp sunflower oil, plus extra
  for shaping

1 lemon, cut into wedges

1. Preheat the barbecue to a moderately
   hot temperature.
2. Pulse the chopped tuna steak in a
   food processor until roughly minced.
3. Add the pecorino, fish sauce, most of
   the chopped parsley and seasoning.
   Pulse again 3–4 more times until just
   incorporated.
4. Remove the mixture from the processor
   and divide into four, then shape into
   patties between oiled hands.
5. Cook the tuna patties on the
   barbecue for 3–4 minutes until lightly
   charred underneath and starting to
   release from the grill.
6. Flip and cook the other side for a
   further 3–4 minutes until the burgers
   are firm yet slightly springy to
   the touch.
7. Remove from the barbecue and serve
   with lemon wedges and more parsley
   on the side.

SERVES: 4 | PREP TIME: 15 MINS | COOKING TIME: 10-14 MINS

Barbecued Whole Fish

4 x 450 g / 1 lb sea bream, gutted and cleaned

110 ml / 4 fl. oz / ½ cup extra virgin olive oil

8 cloves of garlic, finely sliced

1 tbsp red peppercorns

crushed sea salt

1. Preheat a barbecue to a moderately hot temperature.
2. Make 4–5 incisions on each side of the skin of the sea bream.
3. Whisk together the olive oil, garlic and peppercorns, then drizzle over the bream, rubbing the mixture into the incisions. Season with the crushed sea salt.
4. Barbecue the bream for 5–7 minutes on one side, then turn and cook for a further 5–7 minutes until the skin is golden and crisp. The thickest part of the fish should read at least 60°C / 140F on a thermometer.
5. Remove the bream from the barbecue and leave to rest for 5 minutes before serving.

SERVES: **6** | PREP/MARINATE TIME: **1 HOUR** | COOKING TIME: **4 MINS**

Spicy Prawn and Pineapple Skewers

18 raw prawns, peeled with tails left intact
400 g / 14 oz / 2 cup canned pineapple chunks in syrup
2 tbsp butter, melted
1 tsp smoked paprika
½ tsp ground cumin
1 tbsp flat leaf parsley, chopped
1 lemon, cut into wedges

1. Soak six wooden skewers in cold water for 20 minutes.
2. Thread the prawns and pineapple chunks onto the skewers.
3. Mix 50 ml of the pineapple syrup with the butter, paprika and cumin and season with salt and pepper. Brush the mixture over the skewers and leave to marinate for 30 minutes.
4. Cook the skewers over a hot barbecue for 2 minutes on each side or until the prawns are opaque in the centre and lightly charred on the outside.
5. Sprinkle the skewers with parsley and serve with lemon wedges for squeezing over.

SERVES: **4** | PREP TIME: **30 MINS** | CHILLING TIME: **1 HOUR** | COOKING TIME: **30 MINS**

Hot Smoked Salmon

25 g / 1 oz / ⅛ cup sea salt
1 lemon, zest thinly pared, flesh sliced
1 tsp white peppercorns
1 tbsp caster (superfine) sugar
a few sprigs dill
4 portions salmon fillet

1. Put the salt, lemon zest, peppercorns and sugar in a saucepan with 250 ml of water. Stir over a low heat until the salt dissolves, then leave to cool.
2. Put the salmon, dill and lemon slices into the brine, then chill for 1 hour.
3. Set your barbecue up for indirect cooking, so that all of the coals are positioned to one side. Place a metal tray of cold water next to the coals.
4. Toast a cedar plank over the hot coals for 4 minutes, then turn it over and position above the water tray.
5. Remove the salmon from the brine and pat dry. Lay the salmon on top of the plank and top with some of the lemon and dill if you like.
6. Cover the barbecue with a lid and hot-smoke the salmon for 25-30 minutes or until the centre has just turned opaque. Garnish with black pepper to taste before serving.

SERVES: **4** | PREP TIME: **45 MINS** | COOKING TIME: **7-8 MINS**

Grilled Scallop Brochettes

1 large lobster tail, peeled and cut into
4 large chunks

½ small pineapple, peeled and cut into
large chunks

8 queen scallops, roe removed

3 tbsp olive oil

2 large vine tomatoes, halved horizontally

a pinch of dried thyme

salt and freshly ground black pepper

300 g / 10 ½ oz / 2 ½ cups cooked wild
rice, to serve

a small handful of rocket (arugula)
leaves, to garnish

1. Preheat the barbecue to a moderately
   hot temperature and soak four
   wooden skewers in cold water for
   30 minutes.
2. Thread the lobster onto the centre
   of the wooden skewers, with two
   chunks of pineapple and then two
   scallops either side of it.
3. Brush the brochettes with a little olive
   oil and season generously.
4. Brush the tomato halves with a
   little oil before adding thyme
   and seasoning.
5. Grill the brochettes for 5–6 minutes,
   turning once, until the scallops and
   lobster are cooked through and firm
   yet springy to the touch.
6. Remove the brochettes from the
   barbecue and leave them to rest
   while you grill the tomato halves
   for 2 minutes.
7. Serve the brochettes alongside
   the wild rice, rocket and grilled
   tomato halves.

Barbecued Mackerel

1 fresh mackerel per person,
   Horse mackerel or Jack mackerel
   can also be used if available
2 tbsp olive oil
salt and pepper

1. Ensure the fish are gutted and cleaned before cooking.
2. Dry the mackerel thoroughly with kitchen paper, then brush with oil and season liberally with salt and pepper. This will help to prevent them from sticking.
3. Make sure the metal barbecue grill is very hot before adding the mackerel. Cook over medium-hot coals for 4 minutes on each side or until the skin is brown and blistered and the flesh pulls easily away from the bones at the thickest part by the head.

King Prawns with Courgette and Tomato

4 raw king prawns (shrimp)
1 courgette (zucchini), sliced
3 small plum tomatoes, halved
4 tbsp olive oil
crusty bread, to serve

1. Toss the prawns, courgette slices and tomatoes with the oil and season with salt and pepper.
2. Arrange them in an oven-proof frying pan, then sit the pan directly onto the hot barbecue coals.
3. Cook for 5 minutes or until the prawns start to turn opaque and the vegetables turn golden brown. Turn everything over and cook for 3 more minutes.
4. Serve with crusty bread for mopping up the prawn juices.

Grilled Squid

3 tbsp olive oil
2 large preserved red peppers, drained
2 large shallots, finely sliced
3 cloves of garlic, minced
2 green chillies (chilies), finely chopped
salt and freshly ground black pepper
a small handful of flat-leaf parsley, finely chopped
4 squid tubes (thawed if frozen), cleaned and trimmed

1. Preheat the barbecue to a moderately hot temperature.
2. Heat 2 tbsp of the olive oil in a large sauté pan set over a moderate heat until hot.
3. Sweat the red peppers, shallots, garlic and chillies with a little seasoning for 6–7 minutes until softened, stirring occasionally.
4. Stir through the chopped parsley and set to one side.
5. Brush the squid tubes with the rest of the olive oil and season generously.
6. Grill on the barbecue for 2–3 minutes, then flip and top with the sweated vegetable mixture.
7. Continue to cook for a further minute before removing from the barbecue.
8. Serve immediately for best results.

SERVES: **4** | PREP TIME: **10-15 MINS** | COOKING TIME: **35-40 MINS**

Paella

4 large king prawns

2 squid tubes, cut into rings
(thawed if frozen)

75 ml / 3 fl. oz / ⅓ cup olive oil

salt and freshly ground black pepper

1 onion, finely chopped

2 cloves of garlic, finely chopped

1 red pepper, finely diced

300 g / 10 ½ oz / 1 ½ cups paella rice

a pinch of saffron threads

1.25 l / 2 pints 4 fl. oz / 5 cups chicken stock

1 tsp smoked paprika

300 g / 10 ½ oz / 2 cups mussels,
cleaned, with beards removed

150 g / 5 oz / 1 cup clams

75 g / 3 oz / ½ cup firm tofu, cubed

55 g / 2 oz / ½ cup frozen peas

2 lemons, cut into wedges

1. Preheat the barbecue to hot.
2. Brush the prawns and squid with a little olive oil and season generously.
3. Grill for 2–3 minutes, in batches, until the prawns are pink and the squid is starting to brown.
4. Set to one side while you prepare the paella rice.
5. Heat the rest of the olive oil in a large shallow pan and cook the onion and garlic until softened and starting to brown.
6. Add the red pepper and cook for a further 5 minutes, then stir in the paella rice and coat thoroughly in the oil.
7. Stir the saffron into the stock, then pour it over the rice.
8. Add the paprika, stir, bring to a simmer, then simmer uncovered for 20 minutes.
9. Add the mussels, clams and tofu and cook for a further 8–10 minutes until everything is just cooked through and the mussels have opened; discard any that don't open.
10. Return the squid and prawns to the pan along with the peas and leave to warm through for 5 minutes.
11. Adjust the seasoning to taste before serving with lemon wedges on the side.

SERVES: 4 | PREP TIME: **10 MINS** | COOKING TIME: **6-8 MINS**

Barbecued Salmon Steaks

110 ml / 4 fl. oz / ½ cup extra virgin olive oil

a large bunch of flat-leaf parsley

2 tbsp baby capers, drained

1 small shallot, peeled and roughly chopped

1 lemon, juiced and zested

salt and freshly ground black pepper

2 tbsp olive oil

4 x 200–225 g / 7–8 oz salmon steaks

1. Preheat a barbecue to a moderately hot temperature.
2. Pulse together the extra virgin olive oil, parsley, capers, shallot and the lemon juice and zest in a food processor until blended but still chunky.
3. Season to taste and set the salsa verde to one side.
4. Brush the salmon steaks with olive oil on both sides, then season.
5. Cook the steaks on the barbecue for 3–4 minutes on each side until lightly charred and the flesh is firm yet slightly springy to the touch.
6. Serve the steaks immediately with the salsa verde.

SERVES: **4** | PREP TIME: **15 MINS** | COOKING TIME: **12–16 MINS**

Barbecued Swordfish

4 x 250 g / 9 oz swordfish steaks

2 tbsp olive oil

salt and freshly ground black pepper

2 courgettes (zucchinis), sliced

1 aubergine (eggplant), chopped

1 large onion, chopped

1 yellow pepper, sliced

1 red pepper, sliced

1 lemon, thinly sliced

2 tbsp extra virgin olive oil

a pinch of cayenne pepper

a small handful of pea shoots, to garnish

1. Preheat a barbecue to a moderately hot temperature.

2. Brush the swordfish steaks with a little olive oil, then season both sides with salt and pepper.

3. Cook the steaks on the barbecue for 6–8 minutes, turning once halfway through, until they are slightly charred and firm yet springy to the touch.

4. Remove from the barbecue and leave to rest, covered loosely with aluminium foil.

5. Toss the chopped and sliced vegetables and lemon with extra virgin olive oil and a little seasoning, then cook for 6–8 minutes on the barbecue until softened and charred.

6. Pile the swordfish steaks onto plates and top with the vegetables and the lemon.

7. Garnish with a pinch of cayenne and a few pea shoots before serving.

SERVES: **4** | PREP TIME: **40 MINS** | COOKING TIME: **5-6 MINS**

Monkfish Kebabs

1 tsp ground cumin
1 tsp paprika
salt and freshly ground black pepper
2 tbsp sesame seeds
500 g / 1 lb 2 oz / 2 ¼ cups monkfish tail, diced evenly
50 ml / 2 fl. oz / ¼ cup olive oil
a few sprigs of flat-leaf parsley, to garnish
lime wedges, to garnish

1. Preheat the barbecue to a moderately hot temperature and soak four wooden skewers in cold water for 30 minutes.
2. Combine the ground spices with salt, pepper and sesame seeds in a shallow dish.
3. Toss the monkfish pieces in the olive oil until evenly covered.
4. Roll the pieces in the sesame seed mixture, then thread carefully onto the wooden skewers.
5. Arrange on the barbecue and cook for 5–6 minutes, turning frequently, until the fish is firm yet slightly springy to the touch.
6. Remove and arrange on serving plates; garnish with the sprigs of parsley and lime wedges before serving.

Fruit and Vegetable Dishes

MAKES: **12** | PREP TIME: **30 MINS** | COOKING TIME: **15 MINS**

Paneer and Vegetable Skewers

400 g / 14 oz / 2 cups Paneer cheese, cut into chunks

2 courgettes (zucchini), sliced

2 yellow peppers, cut into chunks

24 cherry tomatoes

75 ml / 2 ½ fl. oz / ⅓ cup sunflower oil

1 large shallot, finely grated

2 cloves of garlic, finely grated

1 tbsp fresh root ginger, finely grated

2 tsp chilli (chili) flakes

¼ fresh coconut, grated

1 small bunch coriander (cilantro), finely chopped

1. Soak 12 wooden skewers in cold water for 20 minutes.
2. Thread the Paneer and vegetables onto the skewers and set aside.
3. Mix the oil with the shallot, garlic, ginger, chilli, coconut and coriander.
4. Spoon half of the mixture over the skewers and leave to marinate for 1 hour.
5. Cook the skewers over a medium-hot barbecue for 15 minutes, turning regularly.
6. Drizzle the kebabs with the rest of the marinade and serve immediately.

Courgettes with Chilli Gremolata

4 courgettes (zucchini), halved lengthways
2 tbsp olive oil
1 red chilli (chili), finely chopped
2 tbsp flat leaf parsley, finely chopped
1 clove of garlic, finely chopped
1 lemon, zest finely grated
2 tomatoes, halved to garnish

1. Brush the courgettes with oil and season with salt and pepper. Cook over a medium-hot barbecue for 4 minutes on each side.
2. Mix the chilli with the parsley, garlic and lemon zest and set aside.
3. Transfer the courgettes to a serving board and garnish with the tomatoes. Sprinkle generously with the chilli gremolata and serve immediately.

Grilled Asparagus

350 g / 12 oz / 3 cups asparagus spears, woody ends removed
55 ml / 2 fl. oz / ¼ cup olive oil
salt and freshly ground black pepper

1. Preheat the barbecue to a moderately hot temperature and soak 6 wooden skewers in cold water for 30 minutes.
2. Bunch together four asparagus spears using two wooden skewers threaded across and through them.
3. Brush the spears with olive oil before seasoning.
4. Barbecue for 2–3 minutes on both sides until lightly charred and tender.
5. Remove from the grill and serve immediately for best results.

SERVES: **4** | PREP TIME: **15 MINS** | COOKING TIME: **6-8 MINS**

Portobello Mushroom Burger

110 g / 4 oz / ½ cup plain yogurt
55 g / 2 oz / ¼ cup mayonnaise
a small bunch of chives, roughly chopped
a small bunch of flat-leaf parsley, roughly chopped
salt and freshly ground black pepper
4 Portobello mushrooms, outer skin peeled away and stalks removed
2 tbsp olive oil
4 oat rolls, split
2 large vine tomatoes, sliced
a large handful of rocket (arugula) leaves

1. Preheat the barbecue to a moderately hot temperature.
2. Blitz together the yogurt and mayonnaise in a food processor until smooth.
3. Add the chopped herbs and seasoning and pulse a few times until incorporated, then set to one side.
4. Brush the mushrooms with olive oil and season generously before barbecuing for 6–8 minutes until golden and tender.
5. Spread the bottom halves of the rolls with the herb sauce, then sit the mushrooms on top.
6. Top with tomato slices and rocket before adding the bun tops and serving.

Griddled Aubergines

2 medium aubergines (eggplants)
flaked sea salt
75 ml / 3 fl. oz / ⅓ cup extra virgin olive oil
2 red chillies (chilies), deseeded and
  finely chopped
a small bunch of mint leaves,
roughly torn

1. Preheat the barbecue to a moderately hot temperature.
2. Cut the aubergine lengthways into 2cm (¾ in) thick slices; season with salt and leave to one side for 10 minutes.
3. After 10 minutes, pat the slices of aubergine dry with paper towels.
4. Whisk together the olive oil and chopped chillies, then drizzle over the aubergine, reserving any excess.
5. Cook the slices of aubergine on the barbecue for 2–3 minutes on each side until nicely charred and golden.
6. Remove from the barbecue and serve with the rest of the olive oil and chilli drizzled over and plenty of torn mint on top.

Vegetable Kebabs

1 large aubergine (eggplant), chopped
2 medium courgettes (zucchinis), chopped
12 cherry tomatoes
55 ml / 2 fl. oz / ¼ cup olive oil
salt and freshly ground black pepper
2 tbsp peanuts, crushed

1. Preheat the barbecue to a moderately hot temperature and soak four wooden skewers in cold water for 30 minutes.
2. Thread pieces of aubergine and courgette and two cherry tomatoes onto each skewer, spacing them out.
3. Brush with plenty of olive oil and season generously, then grill on the barbecue for 6–7 minutes, turning occasionally, until softened and lightly charred.
4. Remove from the barbecue and sprinkle with crushed peanuts before serving.

SERVES: **6** | PREP TIME: **30 MINS** | COOKING TIME: **15 MINS**

Garlic and Thyme Veggie Skewers

1 red pepper, cut into chunks

1 green pepper, cut into chunks

1 yellow pepper, cut into chunks

1 red onion, cut into wedges

1 courgette (zucchini), halved and sliced

6 button mushrooms

10 cherry tomatoes

50 g / 1 ¾ oz / ¼ cup butter, softened

2 cloves of garlic, crushed

2 tbsp fresh thyme leaves, plus extra to serve

1 tbsp rosemary leaves, chopped

salt and pepper

1. Soak six wooden skewers in cold water for 20 minutes.
2. Thread the vegetables onto the skewers and set aside.
3. Mix the butter with the garlic, thyme and rosemary. Season with salt and pepper.
4. Brush the skewers with the butter, then cook over a medium-hot barbecue for 15 minutes, turning regularly.
5. Sprinkle the vegetables with a little more thyme and an extra sprinkle of salt and pepper.

SERVES: **4** | PREP TIME: **40 MINS** | COOKING TIME: **12–15 MINS**

Spicy Bean Burger

500 g / 1 lb 2 oz / 2 ½ cups canned
  chickpeas (garbanzo beans), drained
150 g / 5 oz / 2 cups chestnut
  mushrooms, finely chopped
1 tsp dried mint
½ tsp ground cumin
½ tsp ground coriander (cilantro)
½ lemon, juiced
salt and freshly ground black pepper

2 tbsp sunflower oil
4 small sesame seed burger buns, split
2 tbsp tomato ketchup
55 g / 2 oz / 1 cup baby spinach,
  washed and dried
2 tbsp mango chutney
30 g / 1 oz / ½ cup beansprouts

1. Preheat the barbecue to a moderately hot temperature.
2. Cook the chickpeas in a saucepan of simmering water for 15–20 minutes until
    tender, then drain and mash well with the mushrooms, mint, ground spices,
    lemon juice and seasoning.
3. Divide the mixture into four and shape into patties between your hands.
4. Drizzle the patties with sunflower oil then grill for 12–15 minutes until golden
    on both sides.
5. Remove the cooked patties from the barbecue and leave them to cool for a
    few minutes before assembling the burgers.
6. Spread the base of the burger buns with ketchup and top with spinach leaves.
7. Sit the patties on top and spread with mango chutney, then top with beansprouts.
8. Sit the tops of the buns in place before serving.

Barbecued Watermelon Salad

4 wedges watermelon, peeled and sliced

75 g / 2 ½ / 2 ¼ cups mixed baby
 salad leaves

150 g / 5 ½ oz / 1 cup mini mozzarella,
 drained

2 tbsp olive oil

1 lime, juiced

1. Cook the watermelon pieces over a hot barbecue for 2 minutes on each side or until nicely charred.
2. Arrange the salad leaves on four plates and top with the mozzarella and watermelon.
3. Drizzle the salad with oil and lime juice and season with salt and pepper just before serving.

Grilled Pineapple

110 g / 4 oz / ½ cup runny honey

1 vanilla pod, split lengthwise

1 large pineapple, peeled and cored

1 lime, juiced

1. Preheat the barbecue to a moderately hot temperature.
2. Combine the honey and vanilla pod in a small saucepan and warm over a gentle heat.
3. Place the pineapple on its side on a chopping board and cut into rings approximately 2 cm (¾ in) thick.
4. Brush the slices of pineapple with the warmed honey, then grill on the barbecue for 3–4 minutes, turning halfway through cooking.
5. Remove the pineapple from the barbecue and drizzle with a little more honey and some lime juice before serving.

MAKES: **4** | PREP TIME: **25 MINS** | COOKING TIME: **4 MINS**

Fruit Skewers

8 strawberries
8 marshmallows
1 small melon
1 small pineapple

1. Soak four wooden skewers in cold water for 20 minutes.
2. Cut up the melon and pineapple into chunks, ensuring all skin is removed, and remove the tops of the strawberries.
3. Thread the fruit and marshmallows onto the skewers.
4. Barbecue the skewers over the last embers of the fire at the end of the meal for 4 minutes, turning regularly.

Barbecued Bananas

12 small bananas (Lady Finger bananas
  are ideal)

1. Cut a slit down the length of each banana to prevent the skins from bursting.
2. Cook the bananas over a medium-low barbecue for 15 minutes or until the skins
   are charred and crisp, turning occasionally.
3. Delicious served hot with coconut ice cream.

Toasted Marshmallows

150 g / 5 oz / 3 cups assorted
  marshmallows
225 g / 8 oz / 1 ½ cups strawberries

1. Preheat the barbecue to a moderately hot temperature and soak 4 wooden
   skewers in cold water for 30 minutes.
2. Alternately thread the marshmallows and strawberries onto the wooden skewers.
3. Toast the marshmallows by holding them just off the surface of the barbecue,
   turning the skewers to evenly toast.
4. Allow to cool slightly before serving.
5. Delicious served with melted chocolate.

SERVES: **4** | PREP TIME: **10 MINS** | COOKING TIME: **4 MINS**

Pineapple with Lemon Balm

1 bunch lemon balm
125 ml / 4 ½ fl. oz / ½ cup runny honey
1 pineapple, peeled, cored and sliced

1. Reserve a few lemon balm leaves and put the rest in a small saucepan with the honey. Heat gently for 5 minutes to infuse the honey, then strain it through a sieve into a bowl.
2. Brush the pineapple slices with half of the infused honey.
3. Cook the pineapple over a hot barbecue for 2 minutes on each side or until nicely browned.
4. Brush with the rest of the honey and serve hot, garnished with the reserved lemon balm leaves.

Vanilla Glazed Fruit Kebabs

1 star fruit, thickly sliced
2 slices fresh pineapple, cut into wedges
1 banana, sliced with skin left on
1 kiwi fruit, halved and thickly sliced
½ papaya, cut into large chunks
1 pear, halved and thickly sliced
8 strawberries
50 g / 1 ¾ oz / ¼ cup butter
2 tbsp maple syrup
1 vanilla pod, halved lengthways
2 tbsp mixed seeds

1. Soak eight wooden skewers in cold water for 20 minutes.
2. Thread the fruit onto the skewers and set aside.
3. Put the butter and maple syrup in a small saucepan. Scrape the seeds from the vanilla pod and add them to the pan, then warm it gently until the butter melts.
4. Brush half the vanilla glaze over the kebabs, then cook them over a medium-hot barbecue for 4 minutes on each side.
5. Brush the kebabs with the rest of the vanilla glaze and sprinkle with seeds.

Barbecued Nectarines

6 nectarines

1. Cut the nectarines in half and remove the stones.
2. Cook them cut side down on a hot barbecue for 3 minutes, then turn them 90° and cook for another 2 minutes.
3. The nectarines are delicious served hot from the barbecue with ice cream or drizzled with honey.

SERVES: **4** | PREP TIME: **10–15 MINS** | COOKING TIME: **8–10 MINS**

Baked Banana

4 medium, ripe bananas
2 tbsp runny honey, warmed
100 g / 3 ½ oz / ⅔ cup dark chocolate, chopped
100 g / 3 ½ oz / ½ cup fromage blanc or fromage frais
1 tbsp cocoa powder

1. Preheat the barbecue to a moderately hot temperature.
2. Peel the bananas and brush them with runny honey, then wrap them individually in sheets of aluminium foil.
3. Seal the foil to enclose the bananas, then cook them on the barbecue for 8–10 minutes until golden.
4. Remove the bananas from the barbecue and let them cool to one side.
5. Place the chocolate in a heatproof bowl set above a half-filled saucepan of simmering water.
6. Leave the chocolate to melt, stirring from time to time until smooth.
7. Unwrap the bananas and cut them in half.
8. Spoon over some of the melted chocolate and serve with a scoop of fromage blanc on the side, dusted with cocoa powder.

Sides, Sauces and Desserts

SERVES: 4 | PREP TIME: 15 MINS | COOKING TIME: 6-8 MINS

Grilled Halloumi

55 ml / 2 fl. oz / ¼ cup olive oil

2 cloves of garlic

a small bunch of coriander (cilantro)

2 red chillies (chilies), finely chopped

1 lime, juiced and zested

1 tbsp baby capers, drained

100 g / 3 ½ oz / ⅔ cup Kalamata olives, pitted

350 g / 12 oz piece of halloumi, cut into even 2 cm (¾ in) thick slices

salt and freshly ground black pepper

1. Preheat the barbecue to a moderately hot temperature.
2. Pour the olive oil into a mixing bowl, then mince one clove of garlic and finely slice the other. Finely chop most of the coriander.
3. Add the garlic and chopped coriander to the olive oil along with the chillies, lime juice and zest, baby capers and olives.
4. Stir well and add the slices of halloumi; leave to marinate for 5 minutes, then brush off any excess marinade.
5. Grill the halloumi on the barbecue for 4–5 minutes, turning once, until golden and lightly charred on both sides.
6. Season the halloumi with salt and pepper and serve with the olive marinade spooned over and any remaining coriander on top.

SERVES: **4** | PREP TIME: **20 MINS** | COOKING TIME: **18–24 MINS**

Spiced Fries

1.75 l / 3 pints / 7 cups vegetable oil, for deep frying
1 kg / 2 lb 4 oz / 6 cups floury potatoes or sweet potatoes
1 tsp salt
½ tsp paprika
½ tsp ground black pepper
½ tsp caster (superfine) sugar
150 g / 5 oz / 1 cup cornflour (cornstarch)
175 ml / 6 fl. oz / ¾ cup sparkling (seltzer) water, cold
150 g / 5 oz / ⅔ cup barbecue sauce

1. Preheat the oven to 130°C (110°C fan) / 250F / gas ½.
2. Heat the oil in a large, heavy-based saucepan or in a deep fryer to 190°C / 375F.
3. Peel and cut the potatoes into batons and toss with the salt, paprika, pepper and sugar in a large mixing bowl.
4. Whisk together the cornflour and sparkling water to make a simple batter.
5. Working in batches, dip the potatoes into the batter, letting the excess drip off before deep-frying for 6–8 minutes until golden and crisp.
6. Remove and drain on paper towels, then keep warm in the oven as you fry the remaining potatoes.
7. Serve with barbecue sauce on the side.

SERVES: **4** | PREP TIME: **15 MINS** | COOKING TIME: **30-35 MINS**

Smoky Black-eyed Beans

2 tbsp olive oil
75 g / 3 oz / ½ cup smoked bacon, finely chopped
1 large onion, finely chopped
2 sticks of celery, finely chopped
1 large carrot, peeled and finely chopped
salt and freshly ground black pepper
1 tbsp tomato purée
1 tbsp plain (all-purpose) flour
1 bay leaf
600 g / 1 lb 5 oz / 3 cups canned black-eyed beans, drained
500 ml / 18 fl. oz / 2 cups beef stock

1. Heat the olive oil in a large casserole dish set over a medium heat until hot.
2. Sauté the bacon for 3–4 minutes before adding the onion, celery and carrot, then sweat with a little salt and pepper for 5–6 minutes until softened.
3. Stir through the tomato purée and flour. Cook for 1 minute, then add the bay leaf, beans and stock.
4. Stir well and bring to the boil, then simmer gently for 30–35 minutes, stirring occasionally, until the beans are soft and the sauce has thickened.
5. Discard the bay leaf and adjust the seasoning to taste before serving.

Corn with Thyme Butter

4 corn on the cob
1 sprig rosemary
50 g / 1 ¾ oz / ¼ cup butter, softened
1 tbsp fresh thyme leaves
½ tsp dried thyme
½ tsp ground coriander seeds

1. Put the corn and rosemary in a pan of boiling water and cook for 12 minutes. Drain well and discard the rosemary.
2. Mix the butter with the fresh and dried thyme and the ground coriander.
3. Brush half of the butter over the corn then cook on a hot barbecue for 10 minutes, turning regularly.
4. Brush the corn with the rest of the herb butter, then sprinkle liberally with salt and pepper before serving.

Tofu Skewers

350 g / 12 oz piece of firm tofu, cut into bite-sized chunks
1 large courgette (zucchini), halved and cut into half moons
2 medium red peppers, chopped
400 g / 14 oz / 2 cups canned artichoke hearts, drained and cut into chunks
3 tbsp olive oil
salt and freshly ground black pepper

1. Preheat the barbecue to a moderately hot temperature and soak 4 wooden skewers in cold water for 30 minutes.
2. Thread the tofu, courgette, pepper and artichoke hearts onto the skewers, alternating as evenly as possible.
3. Brush with olive oil and season generously.
4. Grill on the barbecue for 7–8 minutes, turning occasionally until the tofu is golden and the vegetables are tender.
5. Remove from the grill and leave to cool slightly before serving.

SERVES: **4** | PREP TIME: **15 MINS** | COOKING TIME: **5-6 MINS**

Barbecued Tempeh

450 g / 1lb / 3 ½ cups tempeh slices

3 tbsp groundnut oil

salt and freshly ground black pepper

150 g / 5 oz / 1 cup raspberries

100 g / 3 ½ oz / ½ cup plain yogurt

75 g / 3 oz / ½ cup wild strawberries, to garnish

a small handful of frisée lettuce, to garnish

250 g / 9 oz / 2 cups cooked long-grain rice, to serve

1. Preheat the barbecue to a moderately hot temperature.

2. Use a round, straight-sided cookie cutter to cut out rounds of tempeh.

3. Brush the rounds with groundnut oil and season with salt and pepper, then grill for 5–6 minutes, turning once, until golden and lightly charred.

4. Blitz two-thirds of the raspberries with the yogurt in a food processor to make a quick sauce.

5. Serve the tempeh with the sauce, with the remaining raspberries, wild strawberries, frisée and rice on the side.

Stuffed Barbecued Peppers

125 g / 4 ½ oz / 1 cup leftover cooked
  vegetables, chopped
1 large egg, beaten
2 tbsp crème fraiche
2 red peppers, halved and seeds removed
2 tsp chopped rosemary
50 g / 1 ¾ oz / ½ cup smoked
  cheddar, grated

1. Mix the vegetables with the egg and crème fraiche and season with a little salt
   and pepper.
2. Stuff the mixture into the peppers, then sprinkle with rosemary and cheese.
3. Set your barbecue up for indirect cooking, so that all of the coals are positioned
   to one side. Place a metal tray of cold water on the other side.
4. Insert the grill and position the peppers on the side of the barbecue with no coals.
5. Put the lid on the barbecue and cook for 20 minutes or until the filling has set
   in the centre.

Spicy Celeriac Oven Chips

1 large celeriac, peeled
4 tbsp sunflower oil
2 tsp smoked paprika
2 tsp garlic powder
2 tsp cracked black pepper

1. Preheat the oven to 200°C (180° fan) / 400F / gas 6.
2. Cut the celeriac into 1 cm (½ in) slices, then cut each slice into 1 cm (½ in)
   wide chips.
3. Boil the chips in water for 5 minutes. Drain well. Leave to steam dry for 2 minutes.
4. Meanwhile, put the sunflower oil in a large roasting tin in the oven to heat for
   5 minutes.
5. Mix the paprika with the garlic powder, pepper and a teaspoon of salt.
6. Sprinkle the mixture over the celeriac and toss gently to coat.
7. Tip the chips carefully into the roasting tin and turn to coat in the oil. Roast for
   40 minutes, turning every 10 minutes, or until light golden brown and crisp.

Barbecued Brie with Courgettes

2 courgettes (zucchini), sliced lengthways
3 tbsp olive oil
1 small ripe Brie
2 tbsp chilli (chili) jam (jelly)
fresh basil, to garnish

1. Brush the courgette strips with oil and season with salt and pepper.
2. Cook the courgettes over a medium-hot barbecue for 1-2 minutes on each side or until nicely marked, then transfer to a hot serving platter.
3. Cook the Brie for 3 minutes on each side or until well-marked, but still holding together.
4. While the Brie is cooking, warm the chilli jam in a small pan over the barbecue.
5. Arrange the Brie in the centre of the platter and drizzle with warm chilli jam. Garnish with basil and serve immediately.

Corn on the Cob

4 corn on the cob (in their husks)
100 g / 3 ½ oz / ½ cup unsalted butter, softened
a small handful of flat-leaf parsley, finely chopped
salt and freshly ground black pepper

1. Peel away the first couple of layers of husk from the corn and soak the corn in a large bowl of cold water for 15 minutes.
2. Preheat the barbecue to a moderately hot temperature.
3. Mix together the butter, parsley and seasoning in a small bowl, then cover and chill.
4. Once the corn has soaked, remove it from the water and pat dry.
5. Half-peel back the remaining husk from the corn, discarding any silk.
6. Cook on the barbecue, turning occasionally, for 12–15 minutes until lightly browned and tender.
7. Remove from the barbecue and spread with the parsley butter before serving.

SERVES: **6** | PREP TIME: **5 MINS** | COOKING TIME: **1 HOUR 45 MINS**

Braised Black Beans

2 tbsp olive oil
1 red onion, grated
3 cloves of garlic, crushed
1 tsp ground cumin
1 tsp ground coriander
½ tsp ground cinnamon
2 tsp ground chipotle
500 g / 1 lb 2 oz / 2 ½ cups black turtle beans, soaked overnight

1. Heat the oil in a large saucepan and fry the onion and garlic over a low heat for 10 minutes, stirring regularly.
2. Stir in the spices and cook for 1 minute, then stir in the beans.
3. Add 1 litre of water, then simmer for 1 hour 30 minutes or until the beans are tender but still holding their shape.
4. Drain the beans of any leftover cooking liquid and season with salt and pepper. Serve with blackened or jerk chicken or any Latin American barbecue dishes.

SERVES: **4** | PREP TIME: **5 MINS** | COOKING TIME: **5 MINS**

Beetroot and Couscous Salad

300 g / 10 ½ oz / 1 ¾ cups couscous
150 g / 5 ½ oz / ¾ cup sunblush tomatoes, plus 3 tbsp of the oil
½ lemon, juiced
½ tsp ground cumin
2 cooked beetroot, halved and sliced
1 handful coriander (cilantro) leaves
grilled halloumi, to serve

1. Put the couscous in a heatproof bowl. Pour over 300 ml of boiling water then cover and leave to steam for 5 minutes.
2. Fluff up the couscous grains with a fork. Whisk the sunblush tomato oil with the lemon juice, cumin and a big pinch of salt, then toss with the couscous.
3. Chop the sunblush tomatoes and fold them through the couscous with the beetroot and coriander.
4. This recipe is delicious served with grilled halloumi.

SERVES: **4** | PREP TIME: **5 MINS** | COOKING TIME: **30 MINS**

Rice, Quinoa and Pepper Salad

250 g / 9 oz / 1 ¼ cups jasmine rice

150 g / 5 ½ oz / ¾ cup red quinoa

750 ml / 1 pint 5 ½ fl. oz / 3 cups chicken stock

2 tbsp olive oil

1 red pepper, diced

1 yellow pepper, diced

1 green pepper, diced

200 g / 7 oz / 1 cup canned kidney beans, rinsed and drained

1 small handful curly parsley, chopped

1. Put the rice, quinoa and stock in a saucepan. When the stock starts boiling, cover the pan, reduce the heat and simmer gently for 10 minutes. Leave to stand off the heat for 15 minutes, without lifting the lid.

2. Meanwhile, heat the oil in a large sauté pan and sauté the peppers and kidney beans for 5 minutes. Fluff up the rice with a fork, then stir it into the sauté pan with the parsley.

3. Serve the rice warm, or chill and serve the same day as a salad. It makes a great accompaniment for Cajun chicken.

SERVES: **4** | PREP TIME: **10 MINS**

Bean Salad

400 g / 14 oz / 2 cups canned cannellini
  beans, drained

300 g / 10 ½ oz / 1 ½ cups canned pinto
  beans, drained

200 g / 7 oz / 1 cup canned black
  beans, drained

2 tbsp white wine vinegar

1 tsp Dijon mustard

a pinch of caster (superfine) sugar

salt and freshly ground black pepper

110 ml / 4 fl. oz / ½ cup olive oil

a small bunch of coriander (cilantro),
  roughly chopped

1 red pepper, diced

1. Combine the drained beans in a large
   mixing bowl and toss well.
2. Whisk together the vinegar, mustard
   and sugar with a pinch of seasoning.
3. Whisk in the oil in a slow, steady
   stream until you have a dressing.
4. Add half of the dressing to the beans
   and toss well, then stir through the
   coriander and pepper.
5. Adjust the seasoning to taste and
   serve with more dressing on the side.

Tomato, Olive and Feta Salad

12 medium tomatoes, cut into wedges

200 g / 7 oz / 1 ½ cups Feta cheese, diced

75 g / 2 ½ oz / ½ cup pimento-stuffed green olives

75 g 2 ½ oz / ½ cup pitted black olives

2 large lettuce leaves, torn into small pieces

1 small handful rosemary tops

1 large handful basil leaves

2 tbsp olive oil

1. Divide the tomatoes between four bowls and top with the feta, olives, lettuce and herbs.
2. Drizzle with oil and season with salt and pepper.
3. Serve immediately.

Potato, Feta and Spring Onion Salad

6 medium potatoes, peeled and cut
  into chunks
4 red spring onions (scallions), sliced
2 tbsp flat leaf parsley, chopped
½ lemon, juiced and zest finely grated
100 g / 3 ½ oz / ½ cup feta cheese,
  crumbled
150 ml / 5 ½ fl. oz / ⅔ cup mayonnaise

1. Put the potatoes in a large saucepan with a teaspoon of salt and cover with cold water.
2. Bring to the boil, then reduce the heat and simmer for 12 minutes or until tender. Drain well and leave to cool.
3. Stir the spring onions, parsley, lemon, and feta into the mayonnaise. Fold in the potatoes and serve at room temperature.

Beetroot, Mozzarella and Walnut Salad

2 medium candy stripe beetroot
50 g / 1 ¾ oz / 1 ½ cups mixed baby
  salad leaves
1 ball mozzarella, torn into pieces
8 walnut halves
2 tbsp walnut oil

1. Put the unpeeled beetroot in a small saucepan and cover with water. Simmer for 30 minutes or until a skewer slides easily into the centre.
2. Transfer the beetroot to a bowl of iced water and leave to cool. Pull off the stalks and slip off the skins, then thinly slice them with a sharp knife or mandolin.
3. Arrange the salad leaves on a serving plate and top with the beetroot, mozzarella and walnuts. Drizzle with walnut oil and season with salt and pepper just before serving.

SERVES: 4 | PREP TIME: 10 MINS | COOKING TIME: 15-20 MINS

Potato Salad

1 kg / 2 lb 4 oz / 6 ⅔ cups new potatoes

1 large shallot, finely chopped

75 ml / 3 fl. oz / ⅓ cup extra virgin olive oil

½ lemon, juiced

a small bunch of flat-leaf parsley, finely chopped

a small bunch of chervil, finely chopped

salt and freshly ground black pepper

1. Cook the potatoes in a large saucepan of salted, boiling water for 15–20 minutes until tender to the point of a knife.
2. Drain and leave to cool before cutting larger potatoes in half.
3. Place the potatoes in a bowl and add the shallot, olive oil, lemon juice, parsley, chervil and seasoning.
4. Stir well to combine; serve warm or cold.

SERVES: **4** | PREP TIME: **20 MINS**

Apple Coleslaw

1 small white cabbage

2 small red onions

4 large carrots, peeled

2 Granny Smith apples, cored

1 royal gala apple, cored

½ lemon, juiced

150 g / 5 oz / ⅔ cup plain yogurt

2 tbsp mayonnaise

salt and freshly ground black pepper

1. Shred the cabbage using a sharp knife, then place in a large mixing bowl.
2. Finely slice the red onion, carrot and apples, then add to the bowl.
3. Add the lemon juice and toss well before adding the yogurt and mayonnaise.
4. Stir well until lightly coated, then adjust the seasoning to taste.
5. Serve immediately or chill until ready to use.

Beetroot Hummus

400 g / 14 oz / 2 ⅔ cups canned chickpeas (garbanzo beans), drained
2 cooked beetroot, quartered
6 tbsp olive oil, plus extra for drizzling
1 tbsp tahini paste
1 tsp sesame oil
1 lemon, juiced
1 clove of garlic, crushed
¼ tsp ground cumin
½ tsp black sesame seeds

1. Put all of the ingredients, except for the sesame seeds, in a food processor and blend until completely smooth. Add a little cold water to get a creamier texture if needed.
2. Season to taste with salt and pepper, then scrape into a serving bowl.
3. Drizzle with oil and sprinkle with black sesame seeds.

SERVES: 6 | PREP TIME: 10 MINS | COOKING TIME: 2 MINS

Crunchy Winter Slaw

1 large carrot, peeled

¼ red cabbage, shredded

¼ savoy cabbage, shredded

½ red onion, thinly sliced

1 small bunch flat leaf parsley, leaves only

2 tbsp pine nuts

1 tbsp pumpkin seeds

1 tbsp sunflower seeds

1 tbsp sesame seeds

1 tsp caster (superfine) sugar

1 lemon, juiced

3 tbsp olive oil

1. Shred the carrot with a julienne tool, mandolin or coarse grater and toss with the cabbages, onion and parsley leaves.

2. Toast the pine nuts in a dry pan for a few minutes until golden brown, then add them to the slaw with the rest of the seeds.

3. Stir the caster sugar and half a teaspoon of salt into the lemon juice to dissolve, then whisk in the oil. Pour the dressing all over the salad and toss well.

Salsa Verde

2 handfuls flat-leaf parsley leaves
1 handful basil leaves
1 handful mint leaves
1 tbsp capers, drained and rinsed
8 anchovy fillets in oil
1 clove of garlic, crushed
½ lemon, juiced and zest finely grated
3 tbsp olive oil

1. Chop the herbs, capers and anchovies together until very fine, then transfer to a bowl.
2. Stir in the garlic, lemon zest, lemon juice and oil, then season to taste with salt and black pepper.
3. Serve as a condiment for lamb chops or fish or use as a marinade for prawns or chicken.

Classic Coleslaw

1 onion, thinly sliced
1 lemon, juiced
2 carrots, peeled
¼ red cabbage, shredded
¼ white cabbage, shredded
1 tsp Dijon mustard
100 ml / 3 ½ fl. oz / ½ cup mayonnaise

1. Put the onion in a bowl with the lemon juice and a pinch of salt. Stir well and leave to macerate for 15 minutes to soften the flavour and texture.
2. Shred the carrot with a julienne tool, mandolin or coarse grater and toss with the cabbages and onion.
3. Stir the mustard into the mayonnaise, then mix the dressing with the shredded vegetables.

Barbecue Sauce

1 tbsp sunflower oil
1 onion, finely chopped
2 cloves of garlic, minced
400 g / 14 oz / 2 cups passata
85 g / 3 ½ oz / ½ cup soft dark brown sugar
2 tbsp distilled vinegar
2 tbsp Worcestershire sauce
salt and freshly ground black pepper

1. Heat the oil in a small saucepan set over a medium heat until hot.
2. Sweat the onion and garlic for 4–5 minutes until soft and golden.
3. Add the passata, sugar, vinegar and Worcestershire sauce and stir well before bringing to the boil.
4. Reduce the heat and simmer gently for 20–25 minutes until completely thickened, stirring occasionally.
5. Season to taste with salt and pepper before serving.

SERVES: **4** | PREP TIME: **40 MINS**

Tomato Salsa

½ small red onion, roughly chopped

a small bunch of coriander (cilantro), roughly chopped

1 lime, juiced

1 tbsp distilled vinegar

a pinch of caster (superfine) sugar

400 g / 14 oz / 2 cups canned chopped tomatoes

salt and freshly ground black pepper

1. In a food processor, pulse together the red onion, coriander, lime juice, vinegar, sugar and a little seasoning until the onion and coriander are finely chopped.
2. Add the tomatoes and pulse again until you have a smoother salsa that still has a little texture.
3. Adjust the seasoning to taste, then cover and chill for 30 minutes.
4. Serve chilled.

Mayonnaise

2 large egg yolks (as fresh as possible)
1 tsp Dijon mustard
salt and ground white pepper
475 ml / 17 fl. oz / 2 cups sunflower oil
1–2 tbsp white wine vinegar

1. Whisk the egg yolks and mustard together in a large mixing bowl.
2. Add a little seasoning and whisk again briefly.
3. Gradually whisk in the oil, drip by drip, for 3–4 minutes until a thick mixture takes shape.
4. After half of the oil has been incorporated, add the white wine vinegar to taste.
5. Continue to whisk in the rest of the oil in a slow, steady stream. Adjust the seasoning to taste.
6. Cover and chill the mayonnaise for up to one week.

Guacamole

½ red onion, finely chopped
2 cloves of garlic, roughly chopped
1 lime, juiced
1 tbsp olive oil
a dash of hot sauce
2 large, ripe Hass avocados, halved,
    peeled and roughly chopped
salt and freshly ground black pepper
tortilla chips, to serve

1. In a food processor, blitz the onion, garlic, lime juice, olive oil, hot sauce and one of the avocados until smooth.
2. Add the remaining avocado and blitz again until smooth.
3. Adjust the seasoning to taste before serving with tortilla chips for dipping.

MAKES: **600 ml** | PREP TIME: **25 MINS** | COOKING TIME: **40 MINS**

Spicy Barbecue Sauce

2 chipotle chillies
3 tbsp olive oil
1 onion, finely chopped
4 cloves of garlic, crushed
2 tbsp fresh root ginger, finely chopped
100 ml / 3 ½ fl. oz / ½ cup pineapple juice
100 ml / 3 ½ fl. oz / ½ cup cider vinegar
100 ml / 3 ½ fl. oz / ½ cup maple syrup
100 ml / 3 ½ fl. oz / ½ cup American style mustard
100 ml / 3 ½ fl. oz / ½ cup molasses
100 ml / 3 ½ fl. oz / ½ cup mango chutney
400 g / 14 oz / 2 cups canned tomatoes, chopped

1. Soak the chipotles in warm water for 20 minutes, then drain well. Remove the stalks and seeds and roughly chop.
2. Heat the oil in a large saucepan and fry the onion and garlic over a low heat for 10 minutes.
3. Stir in the rest of the ingredients plus the chopped chipotles and simmer gently for 30 minutes.
4. Transfer the sauce to a liquidizer and blend until smooth. Leave to cool completely.
5. Use the sauce as a marinade and glaze for ribs, stir into pulled pork or use as a condiment for burgers and chicken.

Chilli and Thyme Finishing Salt

2 tsp black peppercorns
2 tbsp fresh thyme leaves
50 g / 1 ¾ oz / ¼ cup sea salt crystals
2 birdseye chillies (chilies), thinly sliced
1 lemon, zest finely grated
½ tsp smoked paprika

1. Crush the peppercorns with a pestle and mortar, then add the thyme and bruise lightly to release the fragrance.
2. Stir in the rest of the ingredients and then transfer to a small jar.
3. Sprinkle on top of barbecued poultry or fish just before serving.

MAKES: **50 g** | PREP TIME: **5 MINS** | COOKING TIME: **1 MINS**

Spicy Rub for Steaks

1 tsp black peppercorns
1 tsp white peppercorns
1 tsp chilli (chili) flakes
1 tsp smoked paprika
1 tsp dried rosemary
1 tsp dried thyme
1 tsp coriander seeds
2 tbsp sea salt

1. Put all of the ingredients except for the salt in a spice grinder and whizz until roughly ground.
2. Add the salt and whizz again, then tip into an airtight pot and screw on the lid.
3. Use a level teaspoon of rub per steak, rub it in well and leave to marinade for at least 1 hour.
4. You can also add a pinch of rub to softened butter and turn it into butter pats to melt on top of cooked steaks.

Chilli and Garlic Butter for Shellfish

75 g / 2 ½ oz / ⅓ cup butter, softened
2 tbsp brown crab meat
2 red chillies (chilies), finely chopped
2 cloves of garlic, crushed
2 tbsp French tarragon, finely chopped
1 tbsp flat leaf parsley, finely chopped

1. Put all of the ingredients in a bowl with a good grind of black pepper and beat with a spoon to mix.
2. Spread the butter onto halved lobsters, langoustines or king prawns before cooking or add a small spoonful to scallops or oysters cooked in the half-shell.

Blue Cheese and Chive Butter for Steak

75 g / 2 ½ oz / ⅓ cup butter, softened
75 g / 2 ½ oz / ⅓ cup Roquefort
2 tbsp chives, chopped

1. Beat all of the ingredients together in a bowl.
2. Scrape the mixture into the centre of a sheet of greaseproof paper and shape into a large butter pat. Wrap the butter in the paper and chill for at least 1 hour.
3. Slice the butter and melt onto hot steak just before serving.

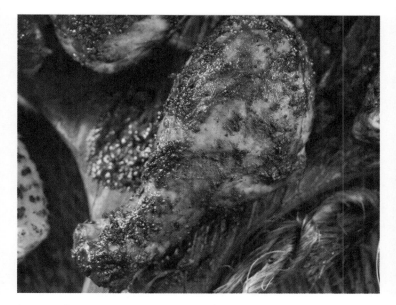

Jerk Marinade

1 tsp sea salt
1 red onion, roughly chopped
1 tbsp root ginger, roughly chopped
2 cloves of garlic, roughly chopped
2 red chillies (chilies), roughly chopped
1 tbsp ground allspice
1 tbsp thyme leaves
1 tbsp dark brown sugar
2 tbsp dark soy sauce
2 tbsp lime juice
2 tbsp orange juice

1. Put all of the ingredients in a food processor and blend to a smooth paste.
2. Scrape the marinade into a large sandwich bag, then add your chicken or pork and massage well to coat.
3. Seal up the bag then transfer to the fridge and leave to marinate for at least 4 hours or overnight.
4. If using bone-in chicken, cook over a medium-low barbecue for 35 minutes, turning regularly, until it is cooked all the way through. It's ready when the juices run clear or when the centre reaches 74°C / 165F on a food thermometer.

SERVES: 8 | PREP TIME: 45 MINS | FREEZING TIME: 4 HOURS

Blueberry Cheesecake

250 g / 9 oz / 1 ½ cups medjool dates, stoned

225 g / 8 oz / 1 ¾ cups walnuts, chopped

250 g / 9 oz / 1 ⅔ cups raw cashew nuts, soaked overnight

400 ml / 14 fl. oz / 2 cup canned coconut milk, chilled unopened

1 ½ lemons, juiced and zest finely grated

75 g / 2 ½ oz ¼ cup runny honey

150 g / 5 oz / 1 cup blueberries

edible flowers to serve

1. Soak the dates in warm water for 10 minutes, then drain and transfer to a food processor. Add the chopped walnuts and pulse until it forms a dough. Line a 20 cm (8 in) round spring-form cake tin with cling film, then press the mixture into the base.

2. Drain the cashews and put them in the food processor.

3. Open the can of coconut milk upside down and discard the thin watery layer. Scoop the thick creamy layer into the food processor and add the lemon juice, zest, honey and half the blueberries.

4. Blend until very smooth, pausing to scrape down the sides occasionally. Scrape into the tin and level the top, then cover with cling film. Freeze the cheesecake for at least 4 hours.

5. Remove from the freezer 20 minutes before serving.

6. Unmould the cheesecake and garnish with the rest of the blueberries and some edible flowers.

Cherry Sorbet

240 g / 14 oz / 2 ⅔ cups cherries, stoned,
plus 4 whole with stalks

1 tbsp stevia sweetener

1 egg white, lightly beaten

1. Put the cherries in the freezer for 3 hours.
2. Transfer the frozen cherries to a food processor. Add the stevia and then add 50 ml / 1 ½ fl oz of water and blend until smooth. Add the egg white and blend again, then scrape the mixture into a plastic tub and freeze for 1 hour.
3. Scoop the sorbet into four glasses and garnish each one with a whole cherry.

Pure Juice Ice Lollies

RED LOLLIES

2 beetroot, quartered

2 red apples, quartered

150 g / 5 ½ oz / 1 cup raspberries

YELLOW LOLLIES

150 g / 5 ½ oz / 1 cup butternut squash,
cubed

1 yellow pepper, quartered

2 mangoes, stoned and cut into chunks

1. For each type of lolly, process the ingredients through an electronic juicer, according to the manufacturer's instructions.
2. Divide each type of juice between two holes of a six-hole ice lolly maker.
3. Freeze for 4 hours or until solid before unmoulding and serving.

SERVES: 4 | PREP TIME: 20 MINS | COOKING TIME: 5 MINS

Fruit Salad

150 g / 5 oz / 1 cup strawberries, halved
125 g / 4 ½ oz / 1 cup blackberries
125 g / 4 ½ oz / 1 cup raspberries
100 g / 3 ½ oz / 1 cup blackcurrants
55 g / 2 oz / ½ cup gooseberries
55 g / 2 oz / ½ cup blueberries
55 g / 2 oz / ½ cup redcurrants
2 tbsp caster (superfine) sugar
a small bunch of mint leaves, picked

1. Combine all the fruit in a large mixing bowl.
2. Spoon over the sugar and toss lightly to coat; leave to sit for 15 minutes, then divide between bowls.
3. Garnish with the mint leaves before serving. It is delicious served with yogurt and honey.

SERVES: 6-8 | PREP TIME: 20-25 MINS | COOKING TIME: 40-45 MINS

Pecan Pie and Vanilla Ice Cream

250 g / 9 oz 1 ¼ cups ready-made shortcrust pastry

a little plain (all-purpose) flour, for dusting

110 g / 4 oz / ½ cup unsalted butter, softened

110 g / 4 oz / ⅓ cup golden syrup

½ tsp vanilla extract

225 g / 8 oz / 1 ⅓ cups soft light brown sugar

3 large eggs

250 g / 9 oz / 2 ½ cups pecan halves

500 g / 1 lb 2 oz / 2 ½ cups good-quality vanilla ice cream

icing (confectioner's) sugar, for dusting

1. Preheat the oven to 180°C (160°C fan) / 350F / gas 4.

2. Roll out the pastry on a lightly floured surface to a large round about 5 mm (¼ in) thick. Use it to line the base and sides of a 20 cm (8 in) straight-sided tart tin.

3. Cut away any overhanging pastry and prick the base all over with a fork.

4. Line the pastry case with greaseproof paper and fill with baking beans before chilling.

5. Melt together the butter, syrup, vanilla extract and sugar in a large saucepan set over a medium heat.

6. Once the sugar has dissolved and the mixture is smooth, remove it from the heat and leave it to cool for a few minutes before beating in the eggs.

7. Blitz the pecans in a food processor, then fold into the sugar and egg mixture.

8. Remove the greaseproof paper and baking beans from the pastry, then pour in the pecan filling.

9. Bake for 40–50 minutes until the pastry is cooked and the filling is set but slightly soft.

10. Remove from the oven and leave to cool in the tin before turning out and cutting into slices.

11. Serve with scoops of vanilla ice cream and a dusting of icing sugar.

Index

Apple Coleslaw 78
Baked Banana 61
Barbecue Sauce 82
Barbecued Bananas 56
Barbecued Brie
  with Courgettes 70
Barbecued Mackerel 42
Barbecued Nectarines ... 60
Barbecued Salmon
  Steaks 45
Barbecued Sardines 35
Barbecued Swordfish 46
Barbecued Tempeh 68
Barbecued Watermelon
  Salad 58
Barbecued Whole Fish .. 38
Bean Salad 74
Beef Ribs in
  Barbecue Sauce 29
Beefburger 14
Beer and Chilli
  Baby Ribs 10
Beer Can Chicken 15
Beetroot and
  Couscous Salad 72
Beetroot Hummus 79
Beetroot, Mozzarella and
  Walnut Salad 76
Blackened Chicken 17
Blue Cheese and Chive
  Butter for Steak 88
Blueberry Cheesecake .. 90
Braised Black Beans 71
Cedar Planked Salmon .. 32
Cherry Sorbet 91
Chicken Kebabs 20
Chicken, Beef and
  Chorizo Skewers 13
Chicken, Sausage and
  Vegetable Kebabs 22
Chilli and Garlic Butter
  for Shellfish 88
Chilli and Thyme
  Finishing Salt 86
Chilli Oil Chicken 24
Classic Coleslaw 81
Corn on the Cob 70
Corn with Thyme Butter .67
Courgettes with
  Chilli Gremolata 51
Crab Cakes 34
Crunchy Winter Slaw 80
Double Lamb Burger 8
Fruit Salad 92

Fruit Skewers 57
Garlic and Thyme
  Veggie Skewers 54
Glazed Duck Breast 21
Griddled Aubergines 53
Grilled Asparagus 51
Grilled Halloumi 64
Grilled Pineapple 56
Grilled Pork Chops 23
Grilled Scallop
  Brochettes 41
Grilled Squid 43
Grilled Toulouse
  Sausages 27
Guacamole 84
Hot Smoked Salmon 40
Jerk Marinade 89
King Prawns with Courgette
  and Tomato 42
Lamb and Beef Skewers .19
Lime and Honey
  Chicken Wings 15
Mayonnaise 84
Mediterranean Chicken
  Sausages 24
Monkfish Kebabs 47
Paella 44
Paneer and
  Vegetable Skewers ... 50
Pecan Pie and Vanilla
  Ice Cream 93
Pineapple with
  Lemon Balm 59
Planked Lemon
  Sea Trout 35
Pork and Beef Burgers 28
Pork Ribs 25
Portobello Mushroom
  Burger 52
Potato Salad 77
Potato, Feta and Spring
  Onion Salad 76
Prawn and Chorizo
  Brochettes 33
Prawn and Scallop
  Skewers 36
Pulled Pork Burger 12
Pure Juice Ice Lollies 91
Rice, Quinoa and
  Pepper Salad 73
Rosemary Chicken with
  Puttanesca Sauce 11
Salsa Verde 81
Shallot and Thyme

Smoked Sausage 20
Sharing Sirloin 16
Shredded Barbecue
  Pork Buns 26
Smoky Black-eyed
  Beans 66
Spiced Fries 65
Spicy Barbecue Sauce ... 85
Spicy Apple
  Chicken Skewers 28
Spicy Bean Burger 55
Spicy Celeriac Oven
  Chips 69
Spicy Prawn and
  Pineapple Skewers 39
Spicy Rub for Steaks 87
Steak 10
Sticky Tomato and
  Herb Ribs 9
Stuffed Barbecued
  Peppers 69
Sweet and Sour
  Chicken Wings 18
Toasted Marshmallows .. 58
Tofu Skewers 67
Tomato Salsa 83
Tomato, Olive and
  Feta Salad 75
Tuna Burger 37
Turkey and Vegetable
  Skewers 16
Vanilla Glazed
  Fruit Kebabs 60
Vegetable Kebabs 53